The Lights in the Darkness

Written by Shareen Wilkinson and Marcus Wilkinson

Illustrated by Alan Brown

Collins

The thing lurks in the garden at night.

In the moonlight, Jaiden and Gabs see a tail quiver ...

They hear a sudden, horrid wail ...

The red pot shatters into bits.

They peek down at the garden.

Is the thing back?

Gabs aims the torch near the shed.

But they cannot see the thing.
It is too quick ...

Back in the bedroom, Gabs and Jaiden hear pattering feet up high.

Lots of cobwebs are hanging down.

11

Orbs appear in the darkness ...

Jaiden and Gabs had disturbed the thing,
hidden deep in its lair.

In the morning, it is back.
That dark fur and quivering tail …

Gabs and Jaiden

12

Hex

6

The thing

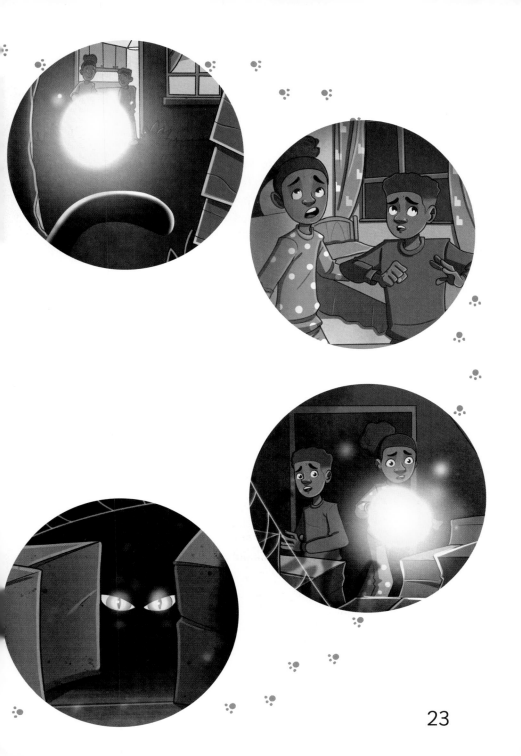

🐾 Review: After reading 🐾

Use your assessment from hearing the children read to choose any GPCs, words or tricky words that need additional practice.

Read 1: Decoding

- On page 2, point to the word **lurks**. Ask: What does it mean? (e.g. *hides, ready to attack*) Discuss the context. Ask: How does the word **lurks** make you feel about the **thing**? (e.g. *scared, nervous*)

- Ask the children to read pages 14 and 15 then say: Listen to the sound I say, point to the word/s that contain the sound. Ask: How is the sound spelled?

  /ar/ (*dark*)   /ai/ (*tail*)   /or/ (*morning*)

- On pages 10 and 11, point to **peek**. Ask: Can you blend in your head when you read this word? Repeat for:

  garden   aims   torch   near

Read 2: Prosody

- Ask the children to read pages 4 and 5 as if they are a storyteller on the radio. Challenge them to use tone and pace to create atmosphere and excitement.

- Discuss which words to emphasise. (e.g. *sudden, horrid wail; shatters*)

- Encourage positive feedback. For example, do they read page 4 slowly, pausing at the ellipsis? Do they try speed up for the action on page 5?

Read 3: Comprehension

- Ask the children if they have read any other stories like this, about a "**thing**"? What was it and what happened?

- Discuss what kind of story this is and why. (e.g. *scary because it's set in the dark, and we don't know what the thing is*)

- Ask the children to retell the story using the pictures on pages 22 and 23.

  o Say: Check that you tell the events in the correct order.

  o Encourage them to use vocabulary from the story. Say: How scary can you make the story sound? What do the characters say?